When I Grow Up

Written by Jo S. Kittinger
Illustrated by Margeaux Lucas

For the Leaky Pens, who helped me become an author
—J.S.K.

To my little nieces, Lauren and Ula
—M.L.

Reading Consultants

Linda Cornwell
Literacy Specialist

Katharine A. Kane
Education Consultant
(Retired, San Diego County Office of Education and San Diego State University)

Library of Congress Cataloging-in-Publication Data

Kittinger, Jo S.
  When I grow up / written by Jo S. Kittinger ; illustrated by Margeaux Lucas.
      p. cm. – (A rookie reader)
  Summary: A young girl contemplates the many things she can be when she grows up, including a truck driver or President.
      ISBN 0-516-23611-3 (lib. bdg.)   0-516-24645-3 (pbk.)
   [1. Growth–Fiction. 2. Sex role–Fiction. 3. Occupations–Fiction.]
   I. Lucas, Margeaux, ill. II. Title. III. Series.
   PZ7.K67152Wh 2003
   [E]–dc21
                                        2003007115

1 2 3 4 5 6 7 8 9 10 R 13 12 11 10 09 08 07 06 05 04

When I grow up,
I can be anything
I want to be.

A doctor.

A farmer.

An artist.

A truck driver.

A singer.

A teacher.

A clown.

A firefighter.

I could even be president.

SEAL of THE PRESIDENT OF THE UNITED STATES

21

**But today,
I just want to play.**

Word List (27 words)

a	doctor	president
an	driver	singer
anything	even	teacher
artist	farmer	to
be	firefighter	today
but	grow	truck
can	I	up
clown	just	want
could	play	when

About the Author

Jo S. Kittinger, a native of Florida, dreamed of becoming an astronaut when she was a little girl. Her strong imagination led to a world of adventures through words. In addition to writing, Jo enjoys nature, pottery, photography, and reading. While teaching her own children to read, Jo realized the critical role of emergent readers. She now lives in Alabama with her husband, two children, and three cats.

About the Illustrator

Margeaux Lucas was born in Ohio, but now resides in New York. She has been drawing constantly since she was four years old, so she always pictured herself an artist. Of course, there were times, while growing up, she thought of other careers like pastry chef or movie star. You will see a lot of her wishes in her illustrations.

ML   12/04